Greetings to OLD CHESHIRE

A WANDER AROUND OLD CHESHIRE
IN EARLY PICTURE POSTCARDS

Catherine Rothwell
and
Cliff Hayes

PRINTWISE PUBLICATIONS LIMITED
1992

© Printwise Publications 1992

Published by Printwise Publications Ltd
47 Bradshaw Road, Tottington, Bury, Lancs, BL8 3PW.

Warehouse and Orders
40-42 Willan Industrial Estate, Vere Street,
(off Eccles New Road),
Salford, M5 2GR.
Tel: 061-745 9168
Fax: 061-737 1755

ISBN No. 1 87226 28 0

Book originated and additional material by

The research and basic work for this book were carried out by Catherine Rothwell and her husband Eddie. Then the book was enlarged and the additional material and captions were added (with Catherine's permission) by Cliff Hayes. So sometimes references to childhood could be either of us.

Manuscript typed and checked Sylvia Hayes.

Printed and bound by Manchester Free Press, Paragon Mill, Jersey Street, Manchester M4 6FP. Tel 061-236 8822.

ACKNOWLEDGEMENTS

The Birkenhead Library; Brian Brittain-Williams; Stanley Buterworth; J. R. Carter, Cheshire County Library; Cheshire Records Office; Chester Public Library; Fryer's of Knutsford; Alice Garnett; Mr and Mrs G. Hicks; Sheila Houghton, H. Mather; Neill McAllister; Kate Milligan; The National Trust; Marilyn Parry; Hazel Pryor; Red Rose Postcard Club; E. G. Rothwell; Rev. Dr. E. J. Rothwell; Ron Severs; St. Christopher's Church, Prestbury; Tourist Information Centres; Birkenhead, Chester. Congleton, Knutsford, Wilmslow; Mr W. D. Trivess; Gertrude Warren; H. D. Forton. (M.D.P.T.A.) Warrington; James Stanhope-Brown, Stretford.

INTRODUCTION

The familiar "tea-pot" shape of Cheshire, with Wirral as spout, Stalybridge-Hyde area as handle, was altered by radical boundary changes in 1974. It has been further modified since, but wherever we wandered in Cheshire most people referred to the old order. The fact that half of Wirral has gone to Merseyside and parts of northwest Cheshire to Greater Manchester will apparently not sink into the mind of the Cheshire traditionalist.

As my husband Eddie and I were collecting information on Old Cheshire, this suited us very well. How amazing it was that the memories of seventy and eighty-year-olds can be so Spring-fresh that the events they relate appear to have occurred but yesterday!, Such immediacy, such total recall can breathe life into an old subject and was invaluable in putting together a book of this kind. We felt not only grateful for this help but inspired by the contacts.

Long strands of connected history involving Celt, Saxon, Roman and Norman settlers inevitably mean a rich inheritance of folklore. We were impressed by accounts of a number of apparently unexplained mysteries, by the distillation of wisdom enshrined in proverbs, weather witticisms and jingles covering the farming year, linking up with ancient customs, some of which, happily, are kept alive today.

As one moves about, a kaleidoscopic impression of the size and diversity of Cheshire emerges: the rich plain stretching from Chester to Congleton; the central sandstone ridge running to Frodsham; the market towns; the seven hill forts; lakes and meres; the gritstone moorland with its stone walls and sheep farms in such contrast to the lush lower meadows with their slowly moving kine. Each place has its own atmosphere. A sense of mystery still clings to the Alan Garner country of Alderley Edge, to Capesthorne and Beeston. Yes, Cheshire's long history has produced a rich heritage but along with this goes the impression of a county poised to step gracefully into the 21st century.

An exciting Cheshire discovery, in 1984, when peat-cutting was in progress on Lindow Moss, "the bogman" was revealed, thousands of years old but preserved from decay because of oxygen-free, waterlogged conditions. Scientists could even tell us, "Lindow Man had eaten bread and porridge before, what was probably, his sacrificial death."

I sincerely hope that these brief glimpses into old Cheshire, may add something to its story and give back some of the pleasure gained in collecting them.

Catherine Rothwell,
1992

ABOUT THE AUTHORS

Once again this unlikely duo combine to produce a book that we hope you will find interesting, informative and nostalgic. Cath with her vast experience as a writer and Cliff with his enthusiasm for history and knowledge of the area.

Catherine Rothwell

Catherine was born in the Prestwich area of Manchester and has resided on the Fylde Coast of Lancashire for the past thirty years. During her career she has been Deputy Borough Librarian of Fleetwood and after re-organisation, in charge of all Local History and Reference for the Lancashire District of Wyre.

Catherine's articles frequently appear in such quality magazines as "Lancashire Life", "The Lady", "Lake Scene" and "Preview of Lakeland".

Her success in writing has led to appearances on B.B.C. and Granada Television, and Catherine has been interviewed on B.B.C. Radio Lancashire, Radio Piccadilly, Coventry and Warwick, Isle of Man Radio and Red Rose Radio. She enjoys lecturing to the W.E.A. and to local Associations and Groups.

Cliff Hayes

Turned from printer (starting on the Widnes and Runcorn Weekly News) to publisher. Cliff now edits and writes more and more, as well as selling the publications. Born in Ellesmere Port (Cheshire) and brought up in Widnes (now in Cheshire), he has a double claim on the area.

Catherine Rothwell

... OF CHESHIRE CATS AND ROSES

Ancient and beautiful Cheshire has been the birth place of many famous people. John Speed, tailor and map maker, was born at Farndon. On a clear day he could see eight counties from Beeston Bluff. Thomas de Quincey referred to the "bonny young women of Altrincham trooping about on market day in their caps and aprons". Ralph Holinshead, the great chronicler of ancient tales of derring-do, came from Sutton, whilst John Gerrard, after studying medicine, achieved fame by travelling as a herbalist and member of the Barber-Surgeons. Charles Kingsley, churchman and author of "The Water Babies", made Cheshire his home for years. Another churchman, Dean Stanley, brought honour to the county as did Wilfred Grenfell for his work in Labrador. James Prescott Joule, scientist, worked in a house in Sale.

Lewis Carroll, whose name is beloved by children everywhere, immortalised the grin of the Cheshire cat in "Alice in Wonderland. The Cheshire cat, which could discourse on pigs and babies, then disappear, leaving only his smile behind, was inspired by the Inn at Stretton. Cheshire cats are wise about weather, washing their ears when rain is on the way and dashing about in storms.

Charles Lutwidge Dodgson, born at Daresbury, learned as a boy to observe animals as others could not do. One local boy who made good, 6ft 4ins. Isaac Podmore, was spotted amongst a Cheshire crowd by the Duke of Cumberland as he moved north in pursuit of fleeing Highlanders. "Fall in!" roared the Duke and Isaac began an army career lasting forty years. In battle he bore a charmed life, soldiering on until he was 90 and returning to his native Styal.

Photo of Lindow bog, Wilmslow.

Fryers Family

Another Cheshire lad who made good in recent years was rose grower Arthur Fryer who started life with a garden shed and half an acre in 1912. Three generations later Fryers of Knutsford, Cheshire, produce one million roses annually. Honour from all over the world have come their way. "Cheshire Life" was the most popular rose of 1974, helping to win for the firm one of the Large Gold Medal Awards at the Southport Flower Show. Frank Fryer, who was born in the Ruskin Rooms in 1919, says of quiet Arthur, the founder, "The old man knew Knutsford when it was nowt. Fields came up to the door and rabbits chased in the great estate of Mere". The obvious thing was to grow roses on the great Cheshire plain. Arthur worked from six each morning to eleven at night. "Roses teach you a lot about life." He believed that the greatest pleasure was to go out on a nice summer morning and see a million roses blooming away. This 1969 picture says it all. Arthur is on the right in a dark jacket; Frank in the deer stalker; Arthur (known as Jim) is the pipe smoker. Peter and Gareth made up the Fryers' name of roses success story, not forgetting the Rolls Royce, which is better to lean on than a garden shed.

Twenty thousand vermillion Cheshire Life roses, gaining Royal patronage and making a great impression at home and abroad in 1982, spoke eloquently for Cheshire county.

SALT, BEECH LEAVES AND CHESHIRE CHEESE

Cheshire salt is well known. A salt pit at Nantwich, mentioned in the Domesday Book, continued to provide the condiment until 1856. Earl Hugh had a Salt House in Northwich in feudal times and despite subsidence the town is still the great home of salt. Nantwich at one time produced three times as much salt as Northwich and Middlewich together. From the brine pit white salt was carried to the wich-houses where great barrels of salt set deep into the earth were filled with salt water. "When the bell ringeth they begin to make fire under the leads; every house has six leads wherein they seethe the said salt water. As it seethes, the wallers (which are commonly women) do, with a wooden rake, gather the salt from the bottom which they put into a long basket of wicker called a salt barrow. The water voideth and the salt remaineth".

In Cheshire, beech leaves were used in place of straw for filling mattresses. According to the diarist John Evelyn, "Besides their tenderness and lying together, they continue sweet for seven to eight years." The leaves came from the beeches of Radnor Mere, reported 300 years old in 1903. Gorse and bracken, more of nature's gifts, was used to keep out the weather by one Cheshire man, Mr Murral and his family, who took up residence in Disley Kirk's cave near Quarry Bank House after the hermit had vacated it. Mad Alan's Hole and Musket Hole are also Cheshire caves once used as dwelling places too.

Gerard, the herbalist already mentioned, declared that the best cheese was made at Nantwich but he was himself a Nantwich man. "Yawning for a Cheshire Cheese" was a game played towards the end of Christmas festivities, after the spiced wassail cup had been handed round. Eggs, honey, spirits and strong ale were part of this recipe, enough to make even the strongest sleepy. The person who could yawn the longest won the Cheshire Cheese.

Cheese making was a strenuous job. Besides being pretty, a good cook, and able to tread the washing in the tub, Cheshire girls were prized for their strong arms, another instance of women doing hard work. The test for a Peover bride was: could she lift the lid off the old oak church chest with one hand?

The Great and Little Pits of Middlewich were dressed on Ascension Day in a ceremony similar to well dressing and upon that day a fair was held. Chester had two great fairs, one at Midsummer lasting three days. By permission of the monks of Stanlow Abbey, stalls and booths thatched with reeds and rushes were set up.

Farm Fold in Styal Village, Cheshire.

PLACE NAMES

The history of Cheshire can be traced in its place names; Wallasey's old name for example, Kirkeby in Waleye, encapsulate nine centuries. When the Scandinavians arrived they found a Celtic church already established but the English had called the area Waleye, meaning "the island of the Welsh".

The Romans occupied Chester for three centuries, and the 20th Legion was sited here. They called it Deva, but its Anglican name Chester comes from Ceaster or the Latin word castra meaning camp. Examples of early Anglican settlements are Altrincham and Warmingham. the "ton" of Bebington means a farm. Characteristic show up in place names e.g. Bickerton (bee keeper's farm) Rode (clearing).

The Vikings invaded Cheshire, the Norse coming from the west via Ireland and the Isle of Man and the Danes from the east. The place name evidence they originated lies in the ending "by" and "hulme" e.g. Cheadle Hulme.

By 1070 the Norman Conquest of Cheshire resulted in a Norman Earldom. All these changes over the centuries are mirrored in many of tell-tale place names in Cheshire townships and manors.

The discharge documents of Roman soldiers found at Malpas and Middlewich show that they were so attracted to Cheshire they decided to settle in it instead of returning to Italy.

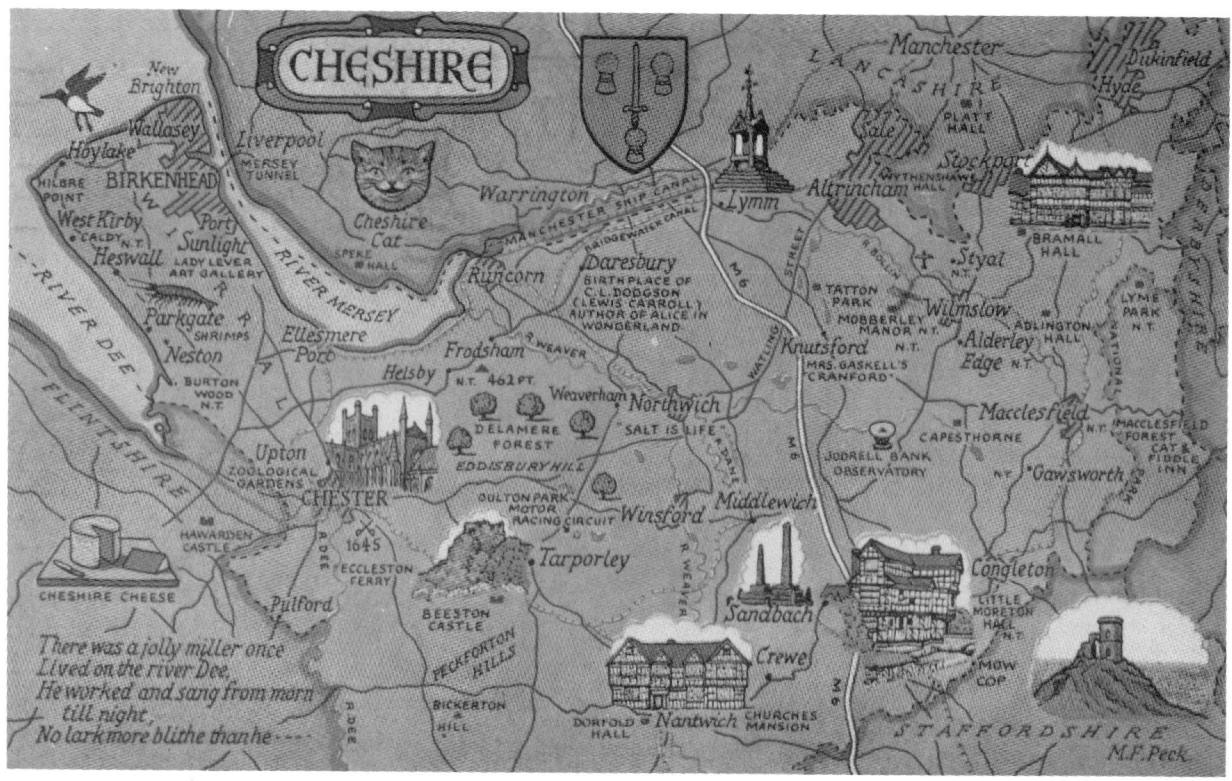

M. F. Peck's delightfully illustrated map of Cheshire accentuating places of interest and those famous County symbols....The Cheshire Cat....Cheshire Cheese.

ALDERLEY EDGE

This 15th century water mill, now owned by the National Trust, was once part of the Nether Alderley estate. At the back is the mill pool from where the water rushes over two mill wheels into a sluice. In the photograph, to the left can be seen a large, old mill stone. The great slope of the roof is composed of stone tiles. For thirty years the machinery lay derelict, but all has now been restored to full working order. Mrs Pamela Ferguson is in charge and occasionally flour is ground for demonstrations. Known as an "overshot tandem wheel watermill", throughout the summer months it receives hundres of visitors who climb its ladder stairs to view.

Alderley Edge used to be referred to as Chorley, the place I best remember there being Artists Lane Nether Alderley, where we stayed in a small, picturesque cottage. I remember the tiny, wild daffodils growing in Spring and meals at Wizard Inn, once known as the Miner's Arms. That name probably arose because quarrying was carried on. Little did I know at that time that the name relates to the legend attached to Alderley Edge.

A wizard attempted to buy a fine, white horse from a farmer who refused the offer. "You will not sell at market," said the wizard, whose words came true. On the way back the farmer again met the wizard who led him into a maze of caverns where countless men and white horses lay sleeping. The farmer's white horse was readily added to the group and he thankfully went on his way rewarded with treasure. Legend has it that the men were King Arthur's warriors "waiting to save their country in some future battle".

This postcard from the 1920s shows a realistic wizard on a white horse outside a cavern, reliving the past. Name of Merlin? On our walks we also found the Wizard's Well with its verse in the rock above:-

"Drink of this and take thy fill
For the water falls by the Whizard's will".

ALTRINCHAM

Pictured in 1914 is the Lancashire and Yorkshire Bank in Atlantic Street, with the Altrincham Free Library and Reading Room above, open 7a.m.-9p.m. each day except Sunday. Further down Atlantic Street, shown in the photograph, was Thornton Pickard where my father worked from 1912 as a photographic apparatus maker. Other works in the area were Schaffer and Budenberg near the Bridgewater Canal and a very famous Linotype factory making linotype machines for the printing industry. The street took its name from George Richard's Atlantic works.

A quaint view of Rostherne Cottages with their thatched roofs, lilac trees and rustic path, posted in 1905 from Altrincham to the far flung outpost of Lime Grove, Timperley telling a Miss Nicholls that the writer couldn't get there and could they meet in Altrincham.

A composite postcard from Valentine's published quickly just after WW2 to satisfy the public making up for 5 years of no holidays or family breaks. The reverse of this states that Ruth is enjoying the peace of the countryside and the rest.

The old Market Place with the fine example of typical half-timbered black and white buildings is shown in this still recogniseable view on a card from just before the first World War issued by Butler's of Altrincham.

ASTBURY

A picturesque post card of Astbury Village and its church, from 1904 showing the village green.

BAGULEY

Baguley is now part of Greater Manchester but this photograph of its station in the 1920s has a rural air. Nothing remains of the buildings and sidings of this once popular station situated at Shady Lane from where trips to the Lancashire coast were run in Holiday weeks. Goods wagons, double track, a classic lamp, old posters and a well-kept railway platform garden take us back to the days of buttoned waistcoats and watch guards as worn by the Railway Company's staff. On the far left stands John Wyatt, station master. A good growing area, Baguley was once renowned for its fine rhubarb known locally as Baguley Beef. Famous seedsmen Clibrans, Dickson, Brown and Tait are associated with it.

BEESTON CASTLE

Beeston Castle, photographed 100 years ago, is seen crowning a rocky eminence above the village of Beeston. Almost impregnable, it was an ideal site, with rock rising sheer on one side and more gentle slopes on the other. Ranulph, Earl of Chester, began building it after his return from the crusades in 1220. In the chief tower was a well of incredible depth. In recent years more than one search has been made for the fabulous treasure which Richard II may have deposited there, but none of the gold or jewels have yet been found. What was a picturesque ruin well over a 100 years ago remains an outstanding county landmark.

BOWDON

Postcard showing Dunham Hill, Bowdon about the turn of the century. This card is easily placed as the cottage is still there today at what is now the traffic lights. Can you imagine car N 246 and its occupants heading for the M56.

BOWDON

Writing to her friend at Bispham House, Bispham, Dora, possibly the lady at the doorway, explains on the reverse of this postcard how busy she has been looking after visitors staying during July in 1905. Many Cheshire tourists lodge at these old thatched cottages at Bowdon. Once the centre of a large parish, Bowdon is now overshadowed by its neighbours Altrincham and Hale, but at the beginning of the century there would be pleasant country and parkland to explore from here. A study of Bowdon's imposing Church, like so many of the fine Cheshire churches, yields much history of the area. The Earls of Warrington, champions of liberty, are commemorated in Bowdon Church.

An even earlier card of the cottages at Rostherne Village, posted 1903 when only the address was allowed on the back.

BRAMALL HALL

Visitors sent home hundreds of these real photographs of "Bramall Hall and Grounds", near Stockport, for friends and relations to stick into postcard albums. This is one of the Grenville Series printed in Petersgate, Stockport. The withdrawing room at Bramall Hall was once described as the most beautiful room in Cheshire.

BRAMALL HALL AND GROUNDS, NEAR STOCKPORT. (No. 1)

One of the finest examples of Antique Timber and Plaster Architecture. Until recently it was the home of the Davenport Family, who resided here since the time of Edward III. The chief object of interest in the interior is the Great Hall with its Oaken Wainscot. The Mantelpiece in the Drawing Room, above which is painted "Vive la Reine," was presented to the Family by Queen Elizabeth.

SIGHTS OF BRITAIN
SERIES OF 48
No. 44
Bramall Hall.

A mile distant from Bramhall Village in Cheshire is this picturesque black and white mansion, dating back some 700 years. For a long period, Bramall Hall belonged to the Davenports. In more recent years it was the home of the Neville family. More recently acquired by the Bramhall Council, certain of its rooms—including the room of Dame Dorothy Davenport, who died in 1636, and who was known throughout England as a great needlewoman—are being furnished in the true style of 300 years ago with authentic pieces of that period, the gifts of local residents.

These Interesting Photographs are issued with the following Cigarettes:—
SENIOR SERVICE....10 for 6d
JUNIOR MEMBER...20 for 1/4
ILLINGWORTH'S No 10... 25 for 1/-

BRAMALL HALL

BRERETON

The Inn in the photograph from the 1960s is the Bear's Head at Brereton, not far from Congleton, built on land that was once part of the estate owned by the Brereton Family. In 1959 quarrying was embarked upon on a large scale as pure silica sand was found. Ten years later this excavation became the lake in Brereton Heath Country Park. This magnificent black and white Inn, situated near the Brereton Hall gatehouse, still has some of its original wattle and daub structure. A bear's head was part of the Brereton family crest.

BOLLINGTON

An interesting story is told about White Nancy which looks down on Ingersley Clough, Bollington, a round, stone tower 220 ft. above sea level, shown in this card from the 1930s. On the reverse the writer states that it was from here that her "Grand-uncle William took the round stone table top and rolled it down the hill. During its descent it cut a hillside cottage in two and finished its journey in the River Bollin. It took eight dray horses and twenty men to get it up again and the cottage had to be repaired so it cost great grandfather Joseph Watts a pretty penny. The stone table is still there."

CAPESTHORNE HALL

The original Hall was destroyed in October 1861 in a dramatic fire and rebuilt as seen here in a 1930's card from Studio Camm in Wilmslow. Visitors to this reputedly haunted house could view the treasures built up and collected by the Davenport family. It is well worth a visit today.

CHESTER

Chester Castle, the seat of the Earls of Chester, is photographed in 1898. Originally a timber construction, it was probably built at an angle of the city walls during the Norman era c.1069. The close link with English and Welsh history is reflected in the records of Kings and Princes calling at Chester Castle. Edward I stayed; Queen Eleanor halted on her way to Caernarvon before the birth of the first Prince of Wales. The head of Sir Piers Leigh of Lyme, faithful follower of Richard II, was fixed on one of the turrets of Chester Castle after his king's defeat and imprisonment. James II pleaded with the burgesses of Chester and leading Cheshire gentlemen at this castle but they would not support his policies.

CHESTER

Amongst several black and white Tudor houses God's Providence House, shown in this fine photograph, was rebuilt in 1862 but still retained part of the old frontage dated 1652 — "God's Providence is mine inheritance." This inscription was said to have been placed there because it was the only house to escape the Plague.

Another example, Bishop Lloyd's House, is considered the best surviving black and white house in Chester. Named after George Lloyd, Bishop of Chester 1604-15, it has two richly decorated gables with biblical scenes, the shield of Sodor and Man (George Lloyd had been bishop there), King James I's initials and some very interesting heraldic animals.

The story of God's Providence House is told in a novel of the same name by Mrs Lineaus Banks.

After 600 years the Goblin Tower on the walls of Chester was rebuilt. On this postcard from 1925 it is called Pemberton's Parlour its 17th century title, from the name of a rope maker who used the tower whilst watching his men at work below the walls. A hoard of Saxon pennies was found near this tower and it was proved that they were minted at Chester.

Within the modern city of Chester the air of an ancient walled town lingers. Seen on entering by the East Gate, many half-timbered houses with overhanging fronts, this medley of ancient dwellings reached its greatest distinction in The Rows, a double row of shops, the upper ones having a covered footway reached by steps from ground level. These unique galleries or arcades are possibly built over the ruins of the Roman city. The basement of number 28 Eastgate Street has a mediaeval crypt. The photograph from 1901 shows Watergate Street Row, so named because the tide once came up this far.

23

This Cross and the Rows postcard dates from 1904

CHESTER

This view taken more than 90 years ago by Catherall and Prichard of Chester overlooks the Roodee (or Rood-eye), a 70 acre grassy meadow enclosed on its other side by a curve of the River Dee. The Chester Race Course and Grandstand can be seen. This huge meadow was once covered by water and the name's origin lies in the "rood" or old stone cross which in those days stood on an "eye" or island in the middle of the area. Chester Races in May is the start of the Social Calendar in the area.

Chester Cathedral was once the church of the Abbey of St. Werburgh but there was a church on the site as early as the 10th century. The Norman Undercroft, which can be seen today, dates from the 12th century. In the 13th century, rebuilding of the Cathedral commenced with the Lady Chapel in Early English style, followed by Chapter Houser and Choir Stalls. Modern changes include the Hammer-beam roof installed in the Refectory in 1939 and a Freestanding Bell Tower completed in 1974. Of the thousands of postcards published of The Cathedral, Chester, this one emanated from Boots Cash Chemists and needed a half penny stamp to convey your greetings, unusually it was printed in Saxony.

Splendid views of Chester, obtainable from the encircling walls, have attracted sightseers for centuries. At the northern corner is the Phoenix Tower, pictured here in a postcard from the 1930s. From here in 1645 Charles I watched the defeat of his Cavalier army at Rowton Moor. It was known as the Phoenix Tower because it was used the the Guild of Painters,Glaziers and Stationers whose emblem was a Phoenix. Tourist today know this as King Charles's Tower. Opposite, on the south east corner are the wishing steps, constructed in 1785, which, in order to have a wish granted, one had to run up and down seven times without taking breath. Today's requirments are less demanding: A would-be wisher must run to the top, back to the bottom and then up again. East of Newgate the Romans built the largest amphitheatre so far found in Britain 314 feet by 286 feet.

CHESTER

An unusual card shows the inside of Chester Cathedral before the first world war.

The Anglo-Saxon Chronicles report that the Norsemen "reached a waste city in Wirral, which is called Legceaster." (Chester). These fierce sea warriers settled on the Dee side of the peninsula and must have been amongst the first to sail up the River Dee.

The picture postcard from 1932 features the Queen's Park Suspension Bridge over the River Dee with its notice of construction, 1928. On the farther side can be seen many rowing boats and it is for pleasure sailing rather than commerce that this beautiful river is now used.

CHURCH MINSHULL

A Raphael Tuck postcard of the 1920s shows the Church House, Church Minshull, a town with the typical black and white timbering of Cheshire. By the 1960s this building had become Church Farm. The church itself had to be rebuilt as at one time "the parishioners were unable to attend services in windy weather without peril to their lives." The quiet of a village street in the 1920s is shown here with relics of times past; the old sun dial, a primitive petrol pump and a vintage motor car.

CONGLETON

Congleton, on the River Dane, probably takes its name from 'congl' meaning a bend in the river. Its parish church, St.Peter's, built in 1740, has a fine Georgian interior with galleries, box pews and coats of arms, but the town is best known for its fine Tudor house, Little Moreton Hall, surrounded by a moat. This black and white, half-timbered building perhaps the most perfect in the country, is managed by the National Trust. A classic example, with overhanging gables and intricate pattern work, it has remained virtually unchanged, but owing to severe deterioration it is under repair as we write.

The Ballroom, Morton Old Hall, Congleton, says the inscription, and one can imagine the scene, with the ladies in their taffeta and silk. Also known as the long gallery.

CREWE

In 1841 a few isolated farm houses occupied the site which became Crewe. This engraving shows the Railway Station of the Grand Junction Railway (three lines from Chester, Manchester and Liverpool). The Tea Room where a lavish dinner, tea and ball were held in celebration. Factories having been recently completed, superintendents, clerks, workmen, wives and relatives were all invited. The workmen received four tickets each so that they could bring their friends. Ladies were admitted free of charge to the tea and the ball. Farmers came from miles around. Five tables and two cross-tables groaned with a spread for 500 workmen and their families. Such toasts as "Prosperity and perpetuity to the Grand Junction Railway" were proposed in honour of the men at the top, right down to the workmen. The dining room being 250 feet in length, there was ample room for dancing for 1,500 persons whilst this was going on, villagers were entertained to a fireworks display provided by the Railway Company.

CREWE

This is the erecting shop of the London and North Western Railway Works, in which the engines, constructed in parts, were assembled. In those days Mr F.W. Webb, known world-wide for his "compound" locomotive, was the Chief Mechanical Engineer of the Company. When this photograph was taken, at the turn of the century, Crewe Works, which was entirely traversed by railway lines, occupied 118 acres of ground of which 36 acres was covered by buildings and employed over 7,000 workmen.

DANE VALLEY

The beauty of the Dane Valley is revealed in this postcard from the 1930s when the Cheshire lanes really were lanes. At Northwich the River Dane flows into the River Weaver but most of the valley lies below Mow Cop Ridge where Primitive Methodism was born. Originally called the Daven, the river must have given its name to Davenham whose church was said to stand "in the very middle of Cheshire".

DELAMERE

Delamere Forest near Norley is photographed in the 1940's. At the time of the compilation of Domesday Book it was known as Earl Hugh's forest. Like the King, Hugh wanted his own area in which to hunt wild boar and deer. The chief foresters were powerful men who brutally enforced forest laws. In Delamere Forest were "hays", hedged enclosures where game was driven to be let out in readiness for the hunts. At the Forest Office today can be seem a replica of the Delamere Horn, badge of authority of the Chief Forester

    The parish chest of Lower Peover was hewn out of the solid trunk of an oak tree probably of local wood from Delamere or The Wirral Forests. Appleton church has a similar one, bound with iron, plus three large locks.

DODDINGTON

This fine engraving of Doddington Park is around 150 years old. The building in the background, known as a Folly, may also have been used as a hunting lodge since from the foreground view there is evidence of a hunt and a stag or hind slain. This stone tower has a group of stone knights in armour said to be guarding Sir James Audley who fought with the Black Prince at Poitiers. The headquarters of the Cheshire Hunt are at Tarporley where toasts are drunk at the Swan Inn with its bow windows and iron railings. A similar custom was observed at the Bear's Paw, Frodsham, an even older place. At one time Tarporley churchwardens paid one shilling for the head of every fox, but the huntsmen were against pheasant shooting.

DUNHAM

Present day Dunham New Park with its picturesque Golf Course can boast a prehistoric burial mound topped with some fine specimens of beech trees. The postcard from 1911 shows the entrance to Dunham Park, a great favourite to visit on Sunday School picnics when I was a child. I remember being very impressed by the herd of red deer, the first I had ever seen.

An early card of The Mill at Dunham posted in 1906. Dunham is also shown on the Altrincham cards.

ECCLESTON

Three small parishes, Eccleston, Pulford and Dodleston lie close to the Flintshire boundary but it is worth remembering that Cheshire along with Wirral once included south Lancashire, the greater part of Flintshire and some of Denbighshire. It was the Treaty of Rhuddlan that moved Cheshire's boundary to the Dee. This charming postcard from the summer of 1912 shows the Eccleston Ferry and River Dee. Old river crossings were jealously guarded privileges. Anyone attempting new ferries could be imprisoned in Chester Castle in the days of the Black Prince.

As can be seen, this stretch of the river was a favourite of the Edwardians. The Ferry was then known as "Jimmy th' Boat" and crossed to Ferry Farm. Teas were served at the Iron Bridge.

The second postcard is another example of the paste-over card. This couple were probably found on cards all over England in similar pose. The publishers got the size a little wrong and the couple are too large and dwarf the picturesque lane and timbered house behind them.

EATON HALL

The Eaton Estate is not far from Eccleston Ferry. Eaton Hall, ancestral home of the Grosvenor family, flanks a particularly lovely part of the River Dee. The gardens were relaid and a lake created from the waters of the Dee in 1812 but 1870 saw complete reconstruction at a cost of £600,000 producing this Gothic mansion shown on the postcard. The historian James Croston refers to "the luck of the Grosvenors" who by marriage built up huge estates. Through Mary Davies of Middlesex an important part of London was acquired in the 17th century. Eaton Hall was classed in "Beautiful Britain" in 1898 as "the youngest of English palaces....in the daily life of such a home a well-ordered magnificence lies, to which a feudal prince might have aspired in vain".

FRODSHAM

This postcard and others of the same buildings were sent by patients at the Crossley Sanatorium at Kingswood, Frodsham. This one posted in November 1908 from Sarah Ann, who boasts she has gained a stone since she arrived, and complains they sleep with the windows open, even though it is very frosty. People were sent there from all over the country. For a time it was known as the Liverpool Hospital. During both wars it was used for the recuperation of soldiers.

This peaceful picture postcard scene of the River Weaver near Frodsham in the late 1930s.

The Victorian Traveller's Guide to 19th century England and Wales gives specific instructions on how to reach Frodsham (pronounced "Fratsum" by older locals) from Holyhead and Chester. The Bear's Paw and the Horse Shoe were recommended Inns at which the traveller could stay. On the west side of Frodsham Street were found traces of a Roman road and an alabaster figure.

The canal from Frodsham Bridge to Weston Park was completed in the early 19th century. Of the two inns on the High Street, bear baiting was carried on at the Bear's Paw. The Queen's Head is the other hostelry to be found in this attractive town which still holds a market each Thursday.

GRAPPENHALL

Grappenhall could be hard to date as it has kept its looks more than most villages in Cheshire. It still has its cobble-stoned area in front of the Inn and church, and the village centre remains almost as this 1920 card.

HELSBY

"THE MOUNT" HELSBY

Helsby and its prosperous and solid nature is shown in this strongly built house with towering chimney stacks, the Edwardian "Mount". The sender tells us proudly that it's her Auntie Agnes' house.

HYDE

Market Place, photographed before the First World War. In early times there was no market at Hyde and the inhabitants had to make their way to Stockport. By the 1850's however the market was well established and for about forty years after 1851 half-yearly fairs were held — they consisted of cattle sales and competitions for prizes etc.

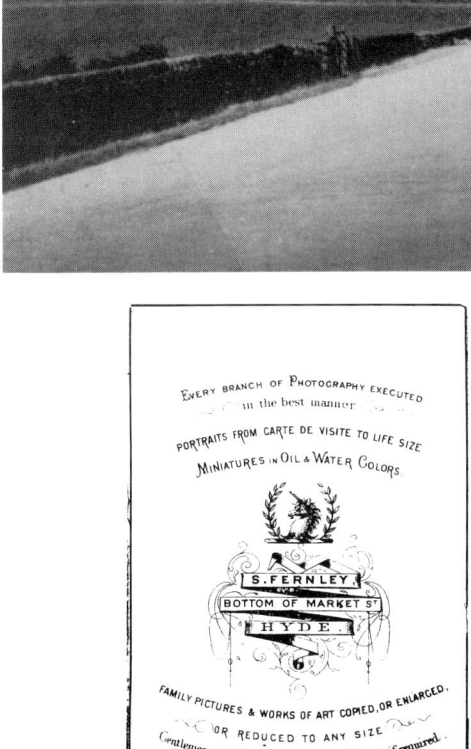

The lonely nature of Hyde is well displayed in this postcard from c.1902, printed in Marple, showing Mottram Old Road. In 1974 a group of Lancashire and Cheshire villages were formed into a new borough centred on the market town of Ashton-under-Lyne. Tameside, as it became known, absorbed Mossley, Stalybridge, Droylsden, Hyde and four other localities.

A phantom dog, yellow in colour, which one lady mistook for a lion escaped from Belle Vue Zoo, Manchester, was seen by a fishmonger from Hyde as late as 1906. He reported that the creature ran alongside him, stopping whenever he stopped and re-starting when he did. This spectre was reputedly sighted in many other places in Cheshire.

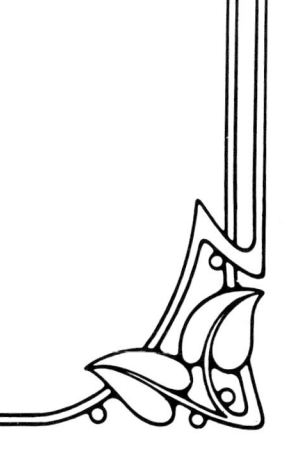

A photographer's card from Hyde.

KNUTSFORD

Knutsford's Heritage Centre, opened in April 1989, was set up in a dilapidated 17th century timber-framed building, once a blacksmith's shop, hidden away amongst courtyards. Knutsford once described as a "marvellous hotchpotch", has a variety of architectural styles ranging from fine Georgian to the Italianate nonsense of Richard Harding Watt. A goodly heritage indeed is the Gaskell Memorial Tower, the former King's Coffee House in King Street, the Ruskin Rooms, the adjoining terraced property of Drury Lane and the merchants' villas in Legh Road. Knutsford nourished the first conservation area in the county outside Chester and its Heritage Centre publicizes the best of the town's traditions; the 127 year old May Day and of course the Knutsford Festival of Sanding.

In 1887, the then Prince and Princess of Wales were so pleased after a special Command Perforamance of the rituals, that they granted a Royal Warrant, to the village.

In recent years the custom of sanding i.e. creating intricate patterns and slogans on the pavements and paths by trickling coloured sand from "tun dishes" (through a funnel) has been associated with May Day, the process commencing early in the morning of May Day, with the May Queen's house being given special attention. A local lady Mrs Leach, points out that at one time sanding was widespread, also done for weddings and other joyous ceremonies. People in those days "sanded" their own premises on May Day.

Ray and Colin Veal, Alf and Jimmy Gilbert are amongst Knutsford's gifted sandmen who take about two days to decorate 50 locations. They naturally pray for fine weather as a deluge would spoil everything. One May Day was remembered for snow, which had to stop before sanding could commence. When Queen Victoria came to Knutsford she was delighted with the sanded streets.

Tabley House, a Palladian mansion standing in beautiful surroundings. Designed by John Carr of York in 1761 for Sir Peter Byrne Leicester. The Regency picture gallery contains a splendid collection of English paintings. Owned by the Victoria University of Manchester and run by the Tabley House Collection Trust the house is open to the public April-October. A lovely place to visit at weekends.

Elizabeth Cleghorn Stevenson, who became the novelist Mrs Gaskell, lived with her Aunt Lumb on The Heath, where Knutsford has long held an annual festival on May Day (the first Saturday in May); indeed Knutsford Royal May Day is famous. The Maypole is set up on the Heath whilst Morris dancers, Jack in the Green and traditional Queen of the May crowning are all features.

Some say that Knutsford got its name because King Canute crossed the River Lily, but it could have once been known as "neats' (cattle) ford", where the cows crossed on their way to market. The postcard from 1906 shows thatched cottages in King Street. The Old Coffee House, the Gaskell Memorial and a 1649 tavern are tourist attractions in the town.

LOWER PEOVER

Lower Peover Church, near Knutsford

Lower Peover Church near Knutsford would be well known to Elizabeth Gaskell, the Cheshire novelist. She had a love of its rural surroundings, and a great dislike of "them nasty cruel railroads" as she refers to the Iron Horse in Cranford. She took the opportunity to make a joke at the expense of fellow novelist Charles Dickens. Captain Brown of Cranford was reading the latest number of Pickwick Papers when a locomotive hit him.

This lovely greetings card is of typical old world Cheshire with its black and white half-timbering, the solid church tower, the huge elm tree and the two pinafored little girls in a deserted country lane before the days of motorised traffic. Lower Peover with its 14th century half-timbering and 16th century stone tower is considered a rare example.

The De Tabley Arms, Lower Peover, taken from the church and showing part of the graveyard. There are a number of Inns of this name showing the influence of the De Tabley family. In 1906 this card thanked Mrs Rowlinson of Rush Green, Lymm for the parcel from a person with the nickname Jimjam.

Lower Peover in a very rural setting on the card used as A Happy New Year Card from January 1905.

45

LYMM

The elegant situation of Lymm's Church of St. Mary is shown in this 20th century postcard. A traditional story connected with Lymm Church describes how an old lady used to fill her bucket from the church spout until one day a hand shot out and dragged the bucket away. Even rain water from the church roof was sacred and not for human use.

Lymm has always been popular as a dormitory town for those engaged in Manchester and Warrington commerce. The town itself has managed to keep its hump-backed bridge over the Bridgewater Canal, its narrow streets, cobbled Pepper Lane and the elaborate 17th century cross next to which are the town stocks shown in the 1908 postcard. The cross, restored in Queen Victoria's Jubilee Year, has steps cut from the outcrop of sandstone on which is stands.

MACCLESFIELD

The postcard from 1931 shows Macclesfield's Market Place, photographed by D. Purdy. The U.C.P. Restaurant and Snack Bar, Boots Chemists with the Bank on the opposite corner were then features here. One of the ancient boroughs of Cheshire, and the administrative centre of Macclesfield Forest, the old town centre has, in modern times, shifted towards Mill Street and Castle Street.

Mary Fitton, Maid of Honour to Elizabeth I, thought to have been Shakespeare's Dark Lady of the Sonnets, lived at Gawsworth Hall, three miles from Macclesfield.

A greeting sent from Macclesfield in February 1910 included; "Kindly see to my box being sent to Lytham station on Friday." A young man touring the country was the writer and he obviously had great faith in the railway's capacity to deliver on time! Steep, winding, cobblestone streets between moss-covered walls are lined with picturesque cottages looking down on the Bollin Valley, although a modern, industrial town has now grown up around the traditional Macclesfield silk mills that dominated when this greeting was sent.

The Church of St. Michael, shown in the postcard stands so high that 108 steps must be climbed to reach it. Its foundation dates from the 13th century, the first church having been built by Queen Eleanor, wife of Edward I Chief events in today's Macclesfield are the May Fair, the bi-annual May Carnival, and the October Wakes Fair.

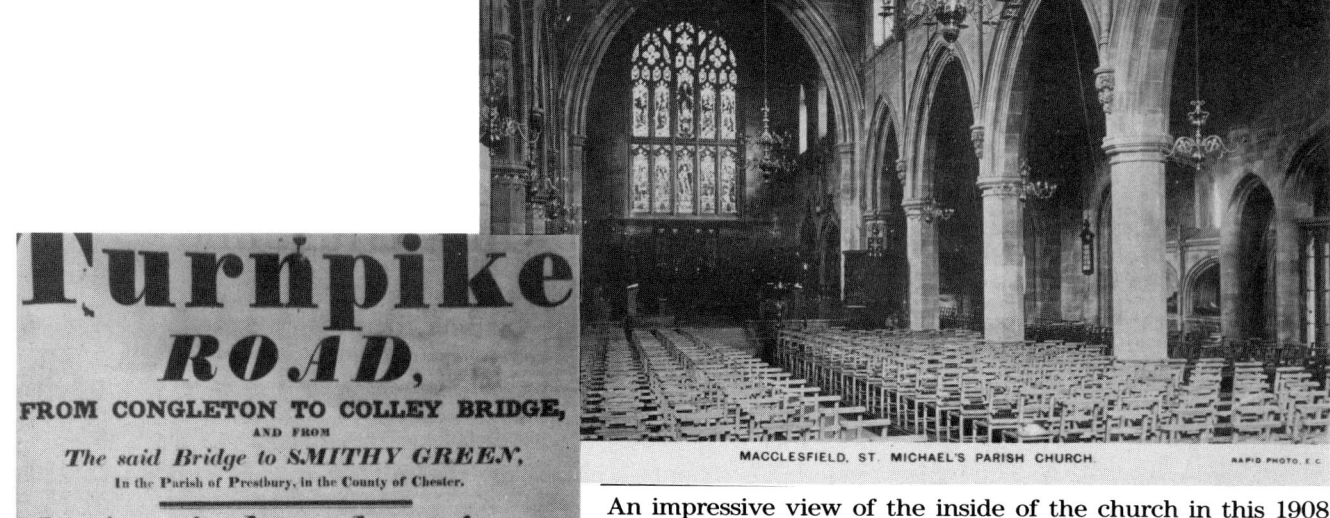

MACCLESFIELD

An impressive view of the inside of the church in this 1908 "RAPID" postcard.

The Turnpike Acts meant that coaches, along with other wheeled vehicles and travellers, had to pay tolls which went towards the upkeep of the highways. This is an interesting poster relating to the road from Congleton to Colley Bridge which shows how Turnpike Trusts could be sold from time to time. Investors considered them a safe and profitable source of income. This auction was held at the Old Angel Inn, Macclesfield. The first Cheshire Turnpike Trusts was formed in 1724.

MALPAS

Malpas Church

Ploughing matches are still held at Malpas each October, one of the few remaining events in England to commemorate the old style of ploughing with shares and heavy horses in pairs. On Plough Monday at least one hand plough was taken into church to be blessed so that the harvest would be bountiful. A Mell supper followed the corn harvest and a potato pie supper was enjoyed after the potato crop had been lifted. Malpas Church, shown in the picture postcard from the 1920s is one of the many fine examples to be found in Cheshire.

MALPAS

On a visit to England the famous American novelist Henry James, writing of Cheshire described "views of a cathedral tower, of waterside fields, of huddled towns and ordered English country...." He thought much of Cheshire damson country and admired the whitethorn and walnut trees that beautified the scene.

Carrying the last load of hay at harvest time, as in this scene from the 1890s, was important all over England but in Cheshire, cutting the last field was more so. A stook of corn tied with blue ribbon was left upstanding and the men threw their sickles, trying to cut the ribbon. The labourer who succeeded was given money by the farmer. Known as "cutting the neck", it derives directly from the Norse word 'neck' meaning sheaf. "cut neck" was the loud shout from the farmworkers before Harvest Supper was eaten.

A lovely coloured card from 1909 shows The Old Cross, with it's unusual crocketed and broach spire, in the village centre, Malpas. It looks like the water cart going away at the top of the street. This is one of a series of cards that were given away free to promote a series of books by Shurey's Publications.

MOBBERLEY

The writer of this fine card of Moberley Church, was kind enough to include the date January 29th, 1904 on the front of the card. At that time Mobberley really was in the heart of the Cheshire countryside, surrounded by leafy lanes.

NANTWICH

"Magpie" houses with blackened timbers and whitened plaster are a typical feature of Cheshire county. The timber for these "Magpie" houses would come from the forests of Delamere, Macclesfield and the Wirral.

Churches Mansion, Nantwich, shown here in all its classic beauty was built in 1577 and was one of the lucky houses to survive the Nantwich Fire of 1583.

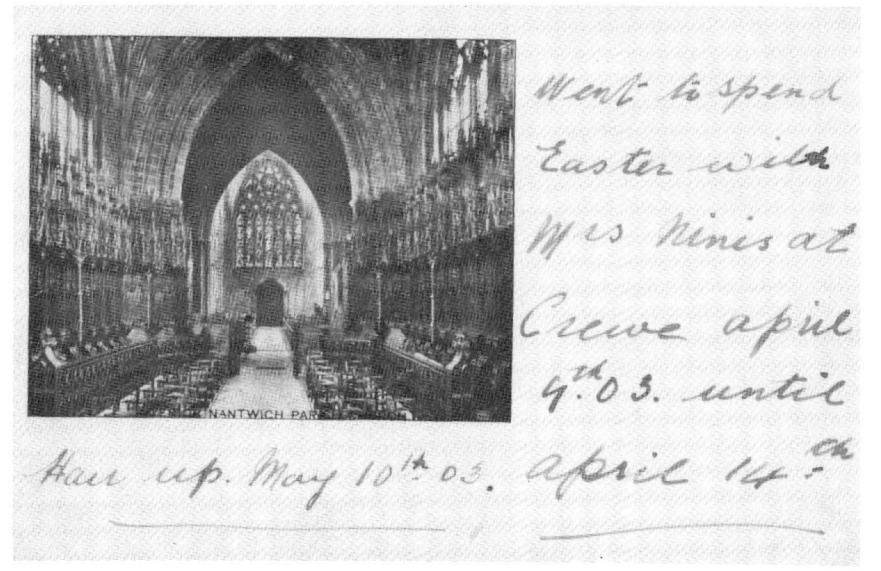

The interior of Nantwich Parish Church is seen on this 1903 greeting card written by a young girl who went to spend Easter at Crewe. She looks forward excitedly to the great event of putting her hair up on May 10th, a practice which at one time denoted that a girl was grown up and ready for marriage. The postcard allowed only the address on the reverse and messages had to be put alongside the photo.

A 19th century Victorian Travellers' Guide describes Nantwich as "standing in a low, flat situation of the east bank of the Weaver. The houses are for the most part old, built of timber and plaster. The Church is large and cruciform with stalls, stone pulpit and octagonal tower. There are several ranges of alms houses. Nantwich was a busy canal centre; the Chester, the Ellesmere, the Liverpool and Birmingham Junction canals and the Middlewich Branch canal all united in the neighbourhood of the town.

NORTHWICH

The motto on Northwich's Coat of Arms means "Salt is life". The vast rock salt beds of Cheshire lie beneath the town and this vital commodity has been exploited since the days of the Romans. 4,000 million gallons of brine a year are extracted and today's chemical industry obtains 75% of its salt supply from Northwich. As one might expect, there is a Salt Museum on Linden Road. This Lilywhite Postcard from the late 1930s shows the Bull Ring, Northwich.

Little of the old town remains to be seen because subsidence caused by salt extraction has demolished buildings. At the turn of the century Northwich High Street was reported to have fell by three feet, adding to the six feet it had fallen in the 1800's. The report from historian Arthur Mee goes on to say "The subsidence, never ceasing is for the most part gradual, but now and then a hole will appear in the ground and part of a house may disappear". A horse and cart once completely vanished. Here is one of the now quite rare postcards showing the subsidence at Dane Bridge, Northwich.

PRESTBURY

Priests House Prestbury has a very colourful past. Shown here in 1930 it was at the time a branch of the District Bank. The name Prestbury comes from the words Priest's House.

Another shot of the Priest's House is included in this combination card from the twenties. Valentine's cards had just brought out the sepia range; nostalgia was the vogue even then.

At Upton Hall, Prestbury, in May 1887 James Croston, a knowledgeable historian on Cheshire completed his monumental work "County Families of Lancashire and Cheshire" and later "Nooks and Corners in Cheshire". He was an authority on the Egertons of Heaton, the Traffords of Trafford, the Grosvenors, Hultons, Harringtons, Bebingtons etc., travelling miles around the county and consulting archives from many sources. One story he recounts is of a duel on February 20th 1685 between Robert Radcliffe,"of haughty, hasty temperament" and Sir Daniel of Tabley. Radcliffe, the last of his line, was killed and the spot from then on was known as Radcliffe's Croft.

Valentine's can always be relied on for their collages and this one from 1950 really does the village proud. I especially like the shot of the Olde Admiral Rodney.

PRESTBURY

The church at Prestbury once was the mother church for Macclesfield and lay at the heart of a great parish. It's building date is uncertain but considered to be between the 13th and 15th centuries. One of the few early burial grounds in East Cheshire was sited here and a Chief Forester of Macclesfield is buried along with notables from many small parishes.

Prestbury was one of the finest rural villages in the whole of Cheshire. This postcard of The Stocks and Church shows the churchyard wall off well. Gawsworth, Sutton, Bosley, North Rode, Marton, Siddington and Henbury were all within the ecclesiastical boundaries of the church and most had inscribed stones set into this wall to show they were involved in the upkeep. Wildboarclough is in there too. During Autumn and Winter the 8 o'clock curfew bell is still rung.

Prestbury Church is also noted for it's Norman Chapel, a small stone building on the south side of the church. In 1953 it was refurnished as a chapel and used for services, having had little use before other than as a family mausoleum. This fine postcard from the Knight collection, 1931, shows the Norman Arch of the chapel on double pillarswhich historians travel far and wide to see for they cannot agree on the identities of the seven figures depicted on the panel above.

RUNCORN

The railway bridge and viaduct at Runcorn was a minor wonder of the age in 1869, glorified in newspapers and later on in postcards. Constructed by the London and North Western Railway Company, the great viaduct over the Mersey shortened the travelling time between London and Liverpool to 5 hours 10 minutes. A mile and a half long, Runcorn viaduct was planned by engineer William Baker, who built the piers on rock. On the Lancashire side were 65 arches and on the Cheshire side 32, of blue Stafford bricks

This view, is taken from the Runcorn side looking towards Warrington. The footpath along the viaduct on the far side proved a convenient substitute for the ferry and signalled the end of the boat trip made famous in Stanley Holloway's monologue "Two-pence per person per Trip."

It's a great shame that the conservation movement hadn't really started when the old transporter bridge was pulled down. It would have made a wonderful tourist attraction, as well as being a short cut. Although taken from the Widnes side it shows The Runcorn bank with the spire of The Parish Church standing out in the mirk of the industrial region, and the two proud bridges in their majestic glory.

SALE

SCHOOL ROAD, SALE.

What a charming scene set in School Road, Sale. The young ladies in their straw boaters chatting on the corner of the cobbled street, with the tradesman obvious by his apron going about his deliveries. Note the three intrepid youngsters obviously fascinated by the camera

SALE

This picture from the 50's showing Sale's last cinema, the Odeon on Washway Road and Ashbrooks the furnishers - an old family owned business, a rarity in these days of big stores and retail parks.

Sale is now swallowed up by Greater Manchester. This genteel card showing Sale in the 1950s and the lovely lawns and yellow lined free road known as The Avenue a prestigious address to have.

Northenden Road, from Sale Station.

A nostalgic looking at Northenden Road look away from Sale Station about the turn of the century.

SANDBACH

Davidson Brothers have produced a fine photograph of St. Mary's Church, Sandbach; this one was sent as a Christmas card on December 23rd 1909. Faith in the Post Office being very strong for delivery in time for Christmas. Situated in the older part of the town above a tributary of the River Wheelock, it was once centre of the parish which stretched as far as Staffordshire. Black and white cottages, a cobbled market square and the proximity of the half-timbered Hall, originally the manor house, add to the atmosphere of antiquity in this Cheshire town. The restored, magnificent Sandbach Crosses were commented on by one William Smith hundreds of years ago: "A man cannot read the writings engraven, except he stands on his head."

ALMS HOUSES, THE HILL, SANDBACH

The second card from Sandbach shows the Alms Houses and the Hill around the time of the First World War. They don't make telegraph poles like that now.

SIDDINGTON

This old postcard of Siddington Post Office is particularly interesting as it shows a thatcher at work on the roof, in those days as common a sight as the muffin man, hurdy gurdy man or the knife grinder. Scarcely a village at all, it has ancient connections in its 14th century church, a one-time Inn the Golden Cross and Siddington Hall. Members of a family called Sydinton fought with the Black Prince at the Battle of Poitiers.

STALYBRIDGE

Stalybridge received its Charter as a County Borough in 1857, but only fours years later was involved in widespread strikes in the cotton industry. This engraving shows Johnson's Mill at Stalybridge when the hands were being called out in a strike which spread, affecting Ashton, Dukinfield, Mottram, Hyde, Newton and Godley, so that in all, 25,000 people were idle. At Bayley's Mill Stalybridge, windows were broken and large doors forced when the workpeople came out into the mill yard. "Places which resounded to the rattle of the shuttle and the loom are given up to silence" reported the Manchester Guardian. "There is not a manufacturing town in which a strike does not rage". Demands were made for "an advance in wages of two shillings per week and a decrease of one hour's time on Saturday." Carpenters, joiners, and bricklayers also wanted better pay and a half day holiday on Saturday.

STOCKPORT

Manchester Road was Stockport's part of the Chester to Manchester route, a Turnpike Road since the 1760s. This Toll House opposite the Hare and Hounds was one of a number set up by the Stockport and Warrington Turnpike Trust in 1821, but it was demolished to make way for a petrol filling station. Beyond the toll gate is 'Ribblesdale', home of a Chairman of the local Parish Council. History is mirrored in the pony and trap, gate, toll house keeper and sett-paved road. In 1851 this small house was occupied by the Jacksons and their ten children.

This postcard dating from the beginning of World War I is endorsed: "In loving memory of James Webb, born April 25 1843 died February 17th 1914 and interred in Cheadle Cemetery." James was an old resident of Stockport. Even at the time of his birth Stockport was a well populated town of 23,000, surpassing Chester's 15,000. An ancient borough created in the year 1220, much of the old town is covered by municipal buildings, the cemetery and a large shopping centre.

At the time when the glass and iron Market Hall and the Museum were built and Vernon Park created by a gang of men from the town Workhouse, Mr Lythgoe, a "professor of aerostatics" went up in a huge, gas filled balloon and travelled as far as Bramhall. This was to mark the laying of a foundation stone for an observation tower but unfortunately the project itself never got off the ground.

Dominated by a 27 arch railway viaduct, Stockport is also noted for having the oldest school in Cheshire, Stockport Grammar School, and an imposing Town Hall with a three-storey clock tower.

STOCKPORT
In Loving Memory
of
James Webb
Born April 25th 1843
Died Feb. 17th 1914

Interred at Cheadle
Cemetery Feb 21st

"Gone but not
Forgotton"

57 Petersburg Rd
Edgeley Park
Stockport

STYAL

Alice Garnett has vivid memories of time spent in Styal Cottage Homes for Children where she arrived late in 1943.

"Myself and two younger sisters settled in Lodge Home. We were given a number (mine was 13) a number to be carefully sewn inside all clothes. We all had our jobs- scrubbing floors patch by patch, polishing door knockers, making beds, doing dishes. One night was darning night, another hair wash night and you couldn't put the brush down until your hair, cut short on entrance into care, was gleaming. Sometimes the siren would go; someone had run away. We had three Home Mothers: Miss Blaikley (she delt out the large spoon of cod liver oil we lined up for each morning); Miss Hurst and Miss Pimlott. Each morning all Homes gathered outside the gates to be led by Mr Dawes on his bicycle, to school. After the war we had the Peace Pageant when all children dressed up in national costume. I liked the Superintendent's office. I remember the raised window where every Saturday we exchanged our pennies for a few sweets. Friday night was picture night, down in the gym, but a real cinema was a very special treat.

There was an orchard at the back of the Lodge House and "midnight creeps" down the polished staircase … to fill a pillow case with gooseberries and apples. One girl dropped the pillow case and the stolen fruit went banging down. All treats stopped, but I believe the boys would have got a beating.

When the day came for release, we sang in time to the train wheels; 'We're going home.'

The 1986 photograph shows Alice, now editor and publisher of Jazz Times, motoring in Cheshire with Mr L.N.Gabbott, owner of the 1928 Austin Seven Chummy.

TABLEY

A postcard from 1909 showing a very sedate and tidy Tabley with the bicycles parked outside the village Inn. Postcard issued by S.Butler of Altrincham.

TARPORLEY

This excellent collage of Tarporley Greetings Cards shows the many types of architecture to be found in this Cheshire village. A Frith series postcard from between the wars.

TATTON

Another of the great houses of Cheshire is Tatton Hall, of which two scenes are shown here, one being an interior, the New Zealand Tree Fernery. The main building, a property of the National Trust, is leased to Cheshire County Council. Created by the Egerton family, the mansion was begun in 1780-90 by Samuel Wyatt and finished by Lewis Wyatt in 1808-13. The third Wyatt brother James also had a hand in designs. Waring of Lancaster made much of the mahogany furniture in the house.

Amongst the delights of Tatton are herds of fallow deer; an arboretum, in Spring ablaze with azaleas; a great avenue of beech trees; a maze; a Japanese garden in which can be seen a Shinto temple imported from Japan in 1910, on an island which is reached by a traditional Japanese bridge spanning Golden Brook. To create this great park the old village, cottages and farms all had to be destroyed, but traces remain as does an earlier timber-framed hall.

TIMPERLEY

What looks like a happy school scene in a pleasant setting about 1911 is Lark Hill, Thorley Lane, Timperley. Previously the home of James Kay, it was one of a number of private schools such as Elizabeth Lawson's on Stockport Road and Robert Crawford's Ladies' School at Egerton Terrace, Timperley. Mary Adshead reigned supreme as Headmistress at Lark Hill until her death in 1920. Altrincham Council bought house and grounds in 1947, leading to tree felling, demolition and today's public park.

Good stabling, a bowling green and pleasure gardens where vines were grown ensured the popularity of the Stonemason's Arms, nicknamed the Naked Child, an Inn dating from 1840. Visible in this photograph, a plaque above the door depicted a child alongside the tools of the mason's trade. Its first landlard was indeed a stonemason who also apprenticed his sons to the trade. In the 1860s the Stonemason's Arms was run by James Platt.

TIMPERLEY

Pickering Lodge, one of the many small country mansions in Cheshire, was built in 1850 by a Yorkshireman from Pickering - hence the name. During World War 1, as can be seen by the wounded soldiers in this 1916 photograph, it was used as a hospital. Local fund-raising efforts helped to provide comfort for the soldiers whilst voluntary staff and V.A.D.s provided the nursing skills. When Timperley Council bought the house in later years it was found to have succumbed to dry rot. Sadly, this pleasant-looking dwelling had to be demolished, leaving only the entrance lodge as a reminder.

One of Cheshire's interesting Inns, the Pelican, probably dates from the time of the Turnpike Trusts. In the mid 18th century several acres of farmland were attached from which the publican harvested the grain with which he brewed his own beer. The view from c. 1912 shows wagonettes outside the Inn, used in popular countryside outings. A few bicycles feature but no motor cars. The new-fangled item was the tram, in those days the delight of my brothers Edward and Charles who lived in the area. The run from Timperley to the Downs became their favourite. The landlord of the Pelican was then Walter Bruton. By 1922 Mr Lister's Timperley Omnibus Company had commenced running.

Stockport Road, Timperley, photographed in 1902, shows Fir Tree Farm on the far right, situated in the 17th century Timperley Common. The Paulden family lived there until 1864 but later that century another family, the Rogersons, took over. A typical black and white, timber-framed dwelling, it was built on top of a low, strong, sandstone wall, some of whose blocks remain today although the farm and the thatched building disappeared in 1928 to make way for shops. The splendid sandstone wall in the foreground ran from Thorley Lane as far as the Hare and Hounds and probably derived from Quarry Bank, Stockport Road.

The Timperley Prize Band used the Dutch Barn at the Hare and Hounds Inn for practice sessions, an Inn of interesting history where meetings of the early township were also held. Dating back to the 18th century when inns were often known solely by the landlord's surname, it was referred to as Goulden's. An old will shows that it once had a loft for a weaving room. The photograph shows the Timperly Brass Band in 1909. Instruments and uniforms were paid for by regular Brass Band Concerts.

WINSFORD

The Smithy Bridge at Winsford shown on a collectable Judge's postcard from the 1930s. When this card was issued Winsford was a busy town with its salt works by the River Weaver. Named after the ford over the River Weaver which separates Over, once a Domesday village, from Wharton, Winsford's population boomed because of its salt trade. It was indeed the centre of the Cheshire salt industry in 1880 but today Northwich with its brine pumps is the busier, although both towns suffered from the bugbear of subsidence.

THE WIRRAL

Although the Wirral was part of old Cheshire it was well covered in our other book "Greetings From the Wirral", but to show I like the Wirral ("I was born near Ellesmere Port" - Cliff), here's a few more cards.

THE WIRRAL

Rough Sea, West Kirby

Swiss Bridge Birkenhead Park. / On Bidston hill. / Hamilton Square Birkenhead / BIRKENHEAD / The Ferry / Old Priory Refectory

Five nice shots of Birkenhead, centred by the magnificent layout of Hamilton Square, started in 1826 and the Town Hall added later in 1887.

WILMSLOW

Still easily recognisable today this fine parade of shops including The Rex Theatre, pictured in this Valentine's card from the 1930's.

```
COLLOTYPE
6 View Letter Card of
WILMSLOW
```

POSTCARD PUBLISHERS USED IN THIS BOOK

We have used postcards from many local publishers/printers and some National ones. The following list mentions the ones where we were able to trace their sources.

Judges Postcards
Valentines
G.D. & D.L.,
Lilywhite Limited
C.E. Adern
J. Salmon Ltd.
Shurey's Publications
The Rapid Photo Printing Co. Ltd
S. Butler, Altrincham
F. Frith & Co. Ltd

W.H. Hodgson, Northwich
Jos. Greaves, Manchester
Atby 7
The Scientific Press Ltd., London
Studio Camm, Wilmslow
Grenville, Stockport
Hugo Lang & Co. Liverpool
British View Cards
Davidson Bros.

If we have left anyone out may we apologise.

LIVE AT CHEADLE

There is a good Train Service to Town, in addition to which there are Twelve Express Motor Buses to and from Town each hour.

The Estate is Thirty Acres in Extent devoted solely to medium sized High-class Houses.

Our Speciality :—ALL HOUSES DIFFERENT.

We have For Sale Detached and Semi-detached Houses with Three and Four Bedrooms, Brick Garages, etc.

CLEAN, WELL LIGHTED ROADS.   Please write for illustrated Booklet.

JAMES B. MILNER & CO.,——Builders
BROADWAY BUILDING ESTATE,
Wilmslow Road,   —   —   CHEADLE.

OTHER BOOKS TO LOOK OUT FOR BY
PRINTWISE PUBLICATIONS LIMITED

MANCHESTER IN EARLY POSTCARDS
(Eric Krieger)
A pictorial reminiscence.
ISBN 1 872226 04 3   £2.50

CHESHIRE 150 YEARS AGO
(F. Graham)
Unique collection of 100 prints of Cheshire in early 1800.
ISBN 1 872226 07 8   £2.99

LANCASHIRE 150 YEARS AGO
Over 150 prints reflecting early
19th century Lancashire.
ISBN 1 872226 09 4   £1.99

BRIGHT AND BREEZY BLACKPOOL
(Catherine Rothwell)
Includes short history of the Tower and the Piers
ISBN 1 872226 13 2   £4.95

SOUTHPORT IN FOCUS
(Catherine Rothwell)
Glimpses of the town's past
ISBN 1 872226 15 9   £2.50

PORTS OF THE NORTH WEST
(Catherine Rothwell)
A pictorial study of the region's maritime heritage
ISBN 1 872226 17 5   £3.95

SUNRISE TO SUNSET
(life story of Mary Bertenshaw)
ISBN 1 872226 18 3   £4.95

GREETINGS FROM OLD SALFORD
(Edward Gray)
A portrait in old postcards
ISBN 1 872226 24 8   £4.95

GREETINGS FROM THE WIRRAL
(Catherine Rothwell)
A portrait in old photographs and picture postcards.
ISBN 1 872226 11 6.   £4.95

OUR OTHER CHESHIRE BOOK AVAILABLE:

THE MANCHESTER MAN
(Mrs. G. Linnaeus Banks)
Re-printed from a 1896 illustrated edition — undoubtedly the finest limp-bound edition ever. Fascinating reading, includes Peterloo. Over 400 pages, wonderfully illustrated.
ISBN 1 872226 16 7   £4.95

POEMS & SONGS OF LANCASHIRE
(Edwin Waugh)
A wonderful quality reprint of a classic book by undoubtedly one of Lancashire's finest poets. First published 1859, faithfully reproduced. Easy and pleasant reading, a piece of history.
ISBN 1 872226 27 2.   £4.95

THE MANCHESTER REBELS
(W. Harrison Ainsworth)
A heady mixture of fact and fiction combine in a compelling story of the Jacobean fight for the throne of England. Manchester's involvement and the formation of the Manchester Regiment. Authentic illustrations.
ISBN 1 872226 29 9.   £4.95

STORIES AND TALES OF OLD MERSEYSIDE
(Frank Hird, edited by Cliff Hayes)
Over 50 stories of Liverpool's characters and incidents PLUS a booklet from 1890 telling of the City's history, well-illustrated.
ISBN 1 872226 20 5   £4.95

STORIES & TALES OF OLD LANCASHIRE
(Frank Hird)
Over 70 fascinating tales told in a wonderful, light-hearted fashion. Witches, sieges and superstitions, battles and characters all here.
ISBN 1 872226 21 3   £4.95

STORIES AND TALES OF OLD MANCHESTER
(Frank Hird, edited by Cliff Hayes)
A ramble through Manchester's history, many lesser known stories brought to life, informative yet human book. Over 50 stories.
ISBN 1 872226 22 1   £4.95

STORIES OF GREAT LANCASTRIANS
(Written by Frank Hird)
The lives of 24 great men of the county told in easy reading style. Complete with sketches and drawings, a good introduction to the famous of Lancashire and Manchester, John Byrom, Arkwright, Tim Bobbins, Duke of Bridgewater.
ISBN 1 872226 23 X   £4.95

MORE STORIES OF OLD LANCASHIRE
(Frank Hird)
We present another 80 stories in the same easy readable style, very enjoyable, great. With special section for Preston Guild, 1992.
ISBN 1 872226 26 4.   £4.95

HOBSON'S CHOICE (THE NOVEL)
The classic and moving story of Salford's favourite tale. Well worth re-discovering this enjoyable story. Illustrated edition.
ISBN 1 872226 36 1   £4.95